Larks, Lanes & Memories

Rosemary Winderlich
Larks, Lanes & Memories

Larks, Lanes & Memories
ISBN 978 1 76041 679 9
Copyright © text Rosemary Winderlich 2019
Cover design: Heidi Rurade

First published 2019 by
GINNINDERRA PRESS
PO Box 3461 Port Adelaide 5015 Australia
www.ginninderrapress.com.au

Contents

I asked my mother	9
Golden road	10
Back road, Clare to Eudunda	11
Border country	12
Whirlwind	13
East from Wilcannia	14
Red roofs of Sydney	15
Return from PNG	16
A unique society: ACT	17
In the mountains	18
Inland silence	19
Adelaide to Ceduna	20
Windmills of Penong	21
On to Yalata	22
Where the whales play	23
Apology or not?	24
Murat Bay Morning	25
Ceduna drought	26
A place name song (sweet music to me)	27
Wheeled world	28
Camp near Goog's track	29
Towards Coober Pedy	30
Drifting Sand	31
On the Oodnadatta track	32
Following pioneers	34
Near Chambers Pillar	35
Night at Palm Valley	36
Hermannsburg	37
Kakadu Waters	38
Ubirr	39

Yellow Waters	40
Nourlangie to Narwarlanga	41
Evening on Ubirr	42
Off again: Adelaide to Brisbane by backtracks	43
In search of a Spiralling Lark	44
Blue Hills	45
New country	46
Leaving Louth	47
Bourke passed by	48
Shadows across the road	49
Another name song	50
Rain at Cairns, just back from PNG	51
Shades of grey	52
At Palm Beach	53
Between again	54
Familiar birdsong	55
Soft country	56
Divided Loyalty	57
Nindigully on the Moonie River	58
Roadkill	59
Dareel to Dingadee	60
On the road agam	61
Near Karoonda	62
Passed by	63
Little Desert	64
For a stranger met in Dimboola	65
Between Minyip and St Arnaud	66
Homesteads	67
Lonely Road	68
Tooleybuc	69
Discovering Barham	70
Deniliquin on the Edward River	71

Wet day on Hay Plains	72
Tracking myself on the map	73
An intriguing little lane	74
Heading for Henty	75
Little town	76
Old Woodlorne Homestead	77
Listening near Munyabla	78
A Macreadie	79
Ah, Josephine	80
In search of a stony stream	81
Somewhere north of Beech worth	82
Corryong	83
Here was a church	84
Over the Divide	85
In search of Gold	86
Near Tumbarumba	87
Henty again	88
At Nag Nag Wah campsite	89
Crossroads	90
Mountain Song	91
Reflections	92
The magic of maps	93

I asked my mother

I asked my mother, as children do
What kind of child was I?
She described each child
affirming each…as she did.
This one loved tidiness, and that one, engines
another liked to be with the animals…

There were seven of us then
two younger ones yet to write their story.
What about me? I asked again.

Well, you, dearie,
always wanted to go everywhere
on anything, any way you could.
…and indeed that was my nature.
The wide world called me to go
from my earliest memory
and is still calling now.

My heart is full of dear places
riven by the pain of distance
still bursting with thankfulness
overflowing with the love
the experiences I have known
…and still I yearn to go.

Golden road

Gold, gold
ripe gold
rich and deep
slicing in from setting sun
splashing, washing
golden sheep
golden tufted grasses
golden sweep of pasture.

Down I go
swooping low
into the valley
cold and deep
dark settlements
no sun can reach…
down, down.

The grade changes
road rounds upwards
engine thrusting
up the ranges
into the light
all gold again
caressed
blessed
by long fingers
of late sunlight

Back road, Clare to Eudunda

I'm drunk on hills and trees and reedy waterways
clumped pines encircling sheds and home yards
avenues of sugar gums and slanting dusty lanes
hills crowned with gossiping eucalypts
dry grasses white against new green
curving creek flats green after rain
crumbling ruins
stark lonely chimneys
sentinel pepper trees…

intoxicated with wide fields of grain
fences parading in between
dust drift from machines eternal stitching
patchwork of brown, browns, browns
new-turned earth cool beneath bare feet
and wide sky over all.
I feast on these.

I'll store these memories
towns half glimpsed, nestled in hills
embraced by dusty groves of pines
humming silence, green singing wheat
wayside white oats swaying
caw of crows and distant hum of traffic…
I feast on all of these.

Border country

Thank you, Lord, for this brown country
mulga and mallee and beefwood tree
and supercilious emu
for space filled with nothing much
but sand and stones and sticks and such
for deep inland quietness
the sky just high nothingness
hills red brown, wild hop's rust
plains blue bush, saltbush, red dust…
for sandy creek beds
raw, bare canyons, gnarled gums
for the Red Heart's blood…Sturt's desert pea
mallee and mulga and beefwood tree
and twisted pine
a rugged, red brown country
mine!

We thank you, Lord, for the riches that spill
from the mine-pocked, massacred Fabulous Hill
bloodstone, basalt, beryllium
congretions, conglomerate, chromium
bauxite, zinc, rhodonite
galena's gleam, red garnet's glow
from the twisting, torrid world below
azurite, aluminium…and on, ad infinitum…
for sparkling quartz, poor man's gold
and all treasures the hills of mullock hold.

Finished? No, there are riches more
in the old hill's deep-hidden store.

Whirlwind

Dance on, whirlwind
over the dry grass
bow and pirouette
chuckle as you pass.

Dance on, whirlwind,
over the wide plain
where river beds and dry dams
yearn for rain.

Whirl your misty skirts
over Mundi Mundi Plain
scatter your gifts
dance on again.

Dance on, whirlwind
through the red dust.
As seasons come and go
dance you must.

East from Wilcannia

Leopard tree, elegant and slim
dreamily poised against pale summer sky
languidly drooping her indolent fingertips
disdainful of myall and mallee and pine.
Delicate tracery, grey dappled bark
willowy grace in the hot red dust.

Cobar, Nyngan…country changes
in the distance pale, low ranges
Moonbi mountains against the sky
soft-rounded, mounded, draped in scrub
humped against the clouds they lie.
Down the years from over the sea
Moonbi mountains call to me.

Thrusting on across the plains
now Warrumbungles distant lie
jagged teeth reaching high
currajong and gum clothe foothills
eagles wheel in windy sky.

Inland Australia
…engraved in my heart.

Red roofs of Sydney

Plane homes down on Sydney town
yellow, mellow in the setting sun.

Sydney streets,
skeletal cranes claw the sky
infant boats nest
near Potts point.

Night falls.
Ferry to Manly…dark harbour
wake gold-dusted furrows
lights tiered soft around
Southern Cross above.

We roll across the gap
east…the open sea
swans settle behind North Head.
Ghost gulls gliding low
shepherd us in to Manly quay
lights rippling gold on black satin.

Dim clouds reflect the cities glow…
harbour of stars.

New Guinea far behind.

Return from PNG

My heart sighs
for blowflies
and crows cries…
I've been away
a long
long time!

Inland peace, creep in, seep in
to my bones, my bones, my bones
wash over me.
I've been away a long, long time.

Inland silence…home
after years of seas roaring
rolling, heaving
never sleeping.

Leave me a while
just let me sit…
My bones were made of these
the listening silence
spiralling larks
gum trees.

I've been away a long, long time.

A unique society: ACT

The first Australians travelled here
following seasons, performing rites
feasted on Bogong moths.

Convicts and soldiers came
disturbed Australia's calm
then gold seekers.

Horses escaped and multiplied
inaccessible mountains
became their own.

Wars, refugees, new ideas
Australian language expanded
society diversified…

and then, from many lands they came
to labour on the Snowy scheme.
Stayed, enriching us

Towns grew here, life changed…
different accents, unfamiliar foods
rewrote history

Symbol of this area's unique character…
wild horses of Adaminaby
roaming free.

In the mountains

This walk beneath trees
will balance the treeless spaces.

Moist autumn air
a rustling under my feet
living ceiling arching over
…this I will store
a feast of green and leaves
for tomorrow's drought
away in the dry country.

My heart's ease…rivers and trees.
When I am weary my heart feeds
on visions of these.

We head over the high plains
warm car world, family contained
singing Settlers' songs
along the Monaro plains
then down
tunnelling under arched branches
dappled shadows patterning the road
down, down, around the mountains
ancient gums enclosing
down to Tumbarumba
leaving the mountains behind us.

Inland silence

Out into the Wimmera morning
heading west for Adelaide from Murtoa
Grampians suspended pale to the south
sleepy Natimuk, wild west shopfronts
and intimate slow stir of small town waking.

West into dusty fields towards sentinel Arapiles
over the hump towards Goroke
tunnelling through dry box avenues.

I stopped by the road near Neuapurr to listen…
inland silence…
sigh of sea in she-oak trees
lazy surf of summer days
my mind away to island shores
still doldrum days and surf slow.

Wind in the she-oaks
sifting back to Riverina summer
long childhood days wandering
to sigh of native pine
and distant caw of crow.

Slow dream of endless days
security and peace
whispering to me here
in Wimmera she-oaks.

Adelaide to Ceduna

The rush as we push the air aside
powering on with relentless drive
cutting the dark with our sword of light
boring a tunnel through the night
probing, dissecting the sleeping plain
crossing light swords with a passing train

on, following the unrolling track
stabbing the silent blanket of black
relentlessly pushing the dark aside
in our onward rush, in our power and pride
Pistons thrust urgently, cogs impelling
tread gripping the bitumen
engine singing a strong round song
boring a tunnel through the night
drawn on by our own sword of light
to the west.

Lights blossom along the road
centre line leads urgently on
where dimming road meets darkening sky
there clouds wide and lowering lie.
Mallee's wind stripped claws whip by
car pursuing, consuming its own light
towards Ceduna, through deepening night.

Windmills of Penong

The windmills of Penong turn round and round
precious water drawn from deep down in the ground.
In the heart beat of the land the past will ever stand
while the windmills of Penong keep turning round.

Wirrangu people travelled these wide plains
followed the seasons on their ancient ways
performed their ancient rites so nature would provide
harvested these low hills and fished these bays.

Through the grass there sighs a gentle breeze
where they camped in the shade of mallee trees
their descendants live here still and I guess they always will
integral part of this community.

The farmers came to grow their wool and wheat
and struggled on through times both sad and sweet
mice plagues, drought, dust…they kept on 'cause they must
struggling together here has built friendships unique.

The windmills of Penong turn round and round
though a newer source of water has been found
pipe line snakes across the sand to water this dry land
still the windmills stand a symbol of this town.

When the windmills of Penong all turn to rust
this community will not dissolve in dust
but grow in strength and peace even though the windmills cease…
life together here has built enduring trust.

On to Yalata

Waves, rolling, crashing in eternally
rolling grey green carpet stretching from the sea
low scrub, remnants of old homes
thorns and rusted iron mark past history.

…on to the west…
turn in from the highway
and here is Yalata community
muted colours, grey country
wide central square for gathering
for inmas, church or gossiping
hidden rhythms, subtle weaving
impossible to appreciate
without years of respectful interaction
time to wait, listen and learn.

Time invested, respect will increase
respect of ways we do not understand
acceptance that undercurrents are there
though we might not see.

Changes will come. Let them come gently
respecting past customs and not reimposing
what outsiders might see as necessary.

We can grow together.

Where the whales play

Wide rolling land
twisted mallee lean away
north from the bight
where breakers roar
seabirds soar
and below cliffs whales play.

Rolling blue bush, saltbush
grey and olive and tan
roll on, roll on to the north
through grey dust country
to the red-dust land.
Precious wilderness
almost untouched by man.

Rugged rocks
and guardian cliffs
stay the might of southern sea.
Below the height
whales calve and play
protected, free.

When we have moved on
will our children still see
from these heights
whales play
in the clear, clean deeps
as we can today?

or will they be only history?

Apology or not?

Once we start, where will it stop?

*My ancestors didn't poison, kill
so why should I apologise, agonise?*
but that was then and this is now
how, how can we deal with our dilemma
smoothed over, glossed over, years pass
deep inside still tensions, distrust…
*I wasn't there, didn't see, can't believe,
heard only respect and sympathy.*
Possibly many didn't know, chose not to know
or stood powerless and shut their eyes
but now…now…what can we do?

Do you churn with the pain of convict children
sent across the world for stealing to live
at parents' pain as children die in degradation
for refugees re-rejected, victims of genocide?
Descendants of many races still grieve and weep
…what is so different here?

We can't ignore the festering sore…open it, clean it
even if your forbears were perhaps innocent
your conscience clean, and it was long ago
still listen to the stories.
Respect the pain.
Suppress automatic defence
say *Yes! I am so sorry, for years of fear
bereft families, lifelong loss and discrimination
I am so sorry*, and grieve together
for those who remember
and for the pain of those long gone.

Murat Bay Morning

Shining morning
sun slow rippling south
golden pathway
to Thevenard across the bay.

Breeze stirs the pines
long shadows retreat
from rising sun
dazzling across wide Murat Bay.

Pigeons rise from the grass
morning revs down
to a slow whirr.

Oyster racks tuck the shallows
pleat the calm sea
slow wrinkling south.

Thevenard's Corinthian columns
stand proud across the water
against sentinel heads.

Hot day coming.

Ceduna drought

Drift-dry desolation
creeping
insidiously infiltrating
through every aperture
undefeatable
enervating

paddock bare
wind ridged
dust ever moving
life blood flowing
going
going…

Quiet sly wind
secretly soil stealing
dust whispering
slipping
sliding
smoking
seeping.

Through the quiet night
lifeblood of a paddock
mother of future crops
moves stealthily through the fence.

A place name song (sweet music to me)

Tallowan, Colona, Nundroo
roads off to Bookaby and Fowlers Bay
Penong, Koonibba and then Ceduna
on through Mudamuckla, Puntabie
Nunjikompita, Wirrula, Yantanabie
Cungena, Poochera, Minnipa, Yaninee
Wudinna just after Pygery
then turn north at Kyancutta.

All these names have stories to tell…
Aboriginal people walking their land
then farmers, struggling hopefully…
of middens, carvings, ruined homesteads
then the partnership of building
roads, railways and water pipeline
…the history of this unique country.

Waramboo, Koongawa, Caralue, Buckleboo
Darke Peak, Waddikee, Karawatha…missed a few
another track angles back again to Karalue
one slants back to Warramboo…
Balugarah Hill, then another track to Waddikee
(and I'm sure I've missed one or two…
must watch out for a flying roo
a wombat or confused emu)
Kimba, then roller coaster to Iron Knob.

T-junction, road right to Whyalla
but we turn north
(one leads left to Gawler Ranges)
Wartaka, Ilaroo then Port Augusta
and turn south at last.

Wheeled world

Purposefully devouring the highway
on we glide, engine singing
wheeled-world warm and familiar.

What are they thinking
those who pass by
in their own worlds
on different ways?

Eyes briefly meeting
minds reach out
then worlds encapsulated
pass into darkness.
Lives with satellite relationships
friends, history
pass and are lost to me…

cogs engage momentarily
then detach
spin off, roll on
as we pass
wondering.

Camp near Goog's track

Long day
scrambling up sand ridges
sliding down the other side
digging out wheels in hot sand
now peace
flat horizon, scribbled mallee
stark silhouetted as sun sinks
deep silence.
Campfire dies.

Silent hours before dawn
black oaks singing unseen
tease predawn emptiness…

silence rudely ruptured by vibrations
thundering train from the west
whistle cutting the dark
lights probing, passing, retreating…

silence more profound.

Campfire circle slowly assembles
morning coffee to dancing torchlight
sizzling steaks – at this hour?

…future memories.

Towards Coober Pedy

North from Adelaide…
evening sunlight gold across the plain
road smooth and straight
striped with fence shadows.

Flinders crouching – mauve-misted
low along the eastern skyline
western hills folded, pleated
rising over the gulf.

Evening sunlight softens harsh hills
air golden over Port Augusta.
Car fights to follow known road west
but we head north today to Coober Pedy.

Every six weeks we made the journey
through the sprawling Gawler Ranges
from Ceduna, north to Coober Pedy
a unique community…white dust, glaring sun
piles of mullock marking shafts.

Outlook Cave…cool, still sanctuary
from white heat…dim, enclosed rooms
colours of earth, sanded smooth
wallpaper of rust-red marbled stone
but I desired an escape route.

Our kind host reserved a room with a window
where, if I woke, I could see out
to a precious square of lighter night.

Drifting Sand

Drifting sand…
invading
all-pervading
whispering sand.

Legions of the innocent
crushed in earth's turning
sigh in the relentless sand
eddying in the wind

forgotten, forgotten.

I hear you.
In ruined, deserted homes
I glimpse children playing.
Solitary pepper tree
heap of tumbled stone
mark your living.

You are part of this land
always with us.
Far echoes of your singing.
are in the whisper of the sand.

On the Oodnadatta track

North towards Alice Springs across the dry and sandy land
visiting historic places on our way
in convoy we follow our forefathers' wagon tracks
rolling on to Hermannsburg, still weeks away.

Corrugations, corrugations
hours bouncing, rattling in perpetual agitation
unceasing, jarring vibrations…
will they never stop!

It's a disgrace, a local says.
We need standardisation.
People out here are the backbone of the nation
they deserve better than these endless corrugations!
When we get to Alice I'll contact the press
register my intention
to proclaim through the nation
a ban on corrugations!

Stony now… *Drat these stones*
they rattle my bones
jolting, bone shaking vibration
on and on and on! he moans.

Ah, at last…
sand, smooth sand
no more vibrations. This is grand
smooth and soothing, no more jarring
swerve and swing – we ride the road
through the dry flat land

*…but this red dust is permeating,
seeping in to everything.
The swaying makes me sick…
and now we're bogged!*

*Will this unending sliding, slipping
gliding never stop?
Oh for a bit of solid ground
or a gravel track
or even corrugations…*

On life's road, my friend, it's much like this.
Soft roads and rocky roads both have their use.
we can't have the smooth without the rough
so hang in there when the going's tough.
There'll be a soft patch soon enough.

Following pioneers

North from Oodnadatta
rivers of rock
dark red glowing
curving flowing
red mulga trees
sun glowing
curled bark
blood-red.

Humped grey saltbush
in a sea of red sand
grass flowing
pale against red stone…
painted desert.

> … and they struggled on
> yearning, hoping
> for a river still months ahead.

End of day – hills darken
from ethereal mauve to blue.
Our long day's drive is over.

> … And how fared they
> oxen slow
> each day an endurance test
> tired eyes ever searching
> for that oasis?

Near Chambers Pillar

Desert oaks
dark against the evening sky
pale angel-blue, mauve and gold
west from Finke

One car is late.
We waited…
now on we rock and rattle
intent on signs…tyre tracks
or dust in air.
Have our party come this way?

Creek beds graced with slender gums
low hills rust-red
stark-silhouetted against darkening sky.
Landscape dims
sun's rays touch cloud ramparts
glowing high.

Not many signposts out here
and hard to see…
They'll be waiting at Chambers Pillar
and the turn-off is near
somewhere.

Is this the right way?

Night at Palm Valley

Warm in my swag, moulded in soft sand
gums etched against darkening sky overhead
quarrelling cockatoos settling for the night
and the stars!
…a rejoicing of stars
layered in navy chiffon
sparkling muted, glowing, retreating
an incredulosity
an immensity of stars!

Moonlight steals in, soothing
luminous ghost gums and silver sand
fire's flare limns humped swags.

Dingo's distant howl
far hoot of owl and sigh of grass
breeze caressing.
Mysterious creak and groan
of night things roaming
beneath cool moon wash
and the immensity of stars.

Hermannsburg

Beside the Finke river bed.
inland wind gently blows
gums rustle
eternal caw of crows.

Around the old church
people sit and wait
to give thanks and praise
to the Lord of our days
for all His blessings here.

Arunta ripples, flows
hymns swell…unique harmonies
blending with sighing wind
in native pines and she-oak trees.

Finke channel
wide and dry
stagnant pools
waiting for rains
flowing slow
through long years.

Kakadu Waters

East Alligator River
water flows sluggishly
roiling, turning
crocodiles waiting unseen.
Sculptured grey-green mudbanks
terraced from the water
the greasy, grey green water.

Low tide…heavy water flows seaward
silvered in morning sun
somewhere far ahead sea breeze
sea roads patterning the water
here…grey-green slow moving
crocodile grey-green, menacing.

Night on the lagoon
water dark dark oil rolling
torch shaft cut, slice, thrust
air cool, calm…water still
small slap slap…
flying foxes rearrange
disturbed birds flap
white moon shine paints paperbark
stark against dark, dark oil rolling.

Boat purring, creeping
light shaft…pierce, probe, dissect
black black and moon white.

Red-eye shine…crocodile.

Ubirr

Ubirr brooding over flood plains.
Wind in pandanus speaking of long years
murmur stirring trees, rising, filling the air
dying, sighing into silence.

Ancient rock walls
carved ageless against the sky.
Under overhanging crags
stories painted…
chronicles of long ago
before the white man came.

Spinifex high on Ubirr
pale gold dancing against red rocks
floodplains undulate to northern horizon
blue and viridian.

Wind whispering
rattling the pandanus
slowly sand smoothing red stone
speaking of long years
breathing through twisted trees
sighing into silence
towards unseen sea.

Afternoon sighs over red rock.
Ubirr sleeps.

Yellow Waters

Vast marshes
water corridors fingering
between trees and reeds
carpets of water lilies
kaleidoscope of birds
rising, wheeling, landing…

brooding crocodile sneering
hunched on her nest
murdering us
with her eyes.

As our boat approaches
pygmy geese pop up like corks
from underwater foraging
fluted lily earphones
turn our way
…eavesdropping.

Crocodile floats close by
bulbous eyes staring insolently
submerges as boat approaches.

Jabiru struts through long grass
smartly suited
lord of the lagoon
and high in a dead tree
sea eagles stand sentinel
carved stark against the sky.

Nourlangie to Narwarlanga

Ancient sentinels
emanate agelessness
brooding over flood plains
to far escarpment.

On the slopes of Narwarlanga
far cry of cockatoos
float through cool air pool
still and deep between
squared granite boulders
haphazardly scattered.

At the feet of Nourlangie
strataed oases, small waterfalls
little stream zigzagging
through weathered rocks
smooth slipping between
slow smoothing, carving as they go
down, down the gully.

Nourlangie Rock…
quiet winds stirring
sparse grasses bending
air vibrating with long ago.

Evening on Ubirr

Ponderous pheasant coucal…
descending whoops
across the swamp

Whistling kite
black wing tips grasp the sky.
soaring free.

Glossy ibis
angled stark against clouds
graceful.

Brolgas
silhouetted against the sky
majestic.

Night sounds of Kakadu.
bird calls unlike southern birds
tropical, exotic.

Silently
magpie geese arrow over.
Evening darkens.

Ubirr – eternal
bold against the sky
guards the flood plains.

Off again: Adelaide to Brisbane by back tracks

The road is calling me
always calling me
has since my first memory…
Yes, the road is calling me.

Up with the sun, the packing's done
ready for today's long run
the tank is full and I feel the pull
of the long road calling me.

Where does this road go? I long to know
what trees grow, what rivers flow
ahead of me as I onward go…
the road is calling me.

Good times spent with friends
old relationships to mend
so I roll out on the track again…
the road is calling me.

In search of a Spiralling Lark

North from Burra
country green and pleasant
I resume my long-deferred search
for a spiralling lark.

We biked three miles to school
distance rich and full
special places, birds and flowers
unfolding mysteries.
Cold winter mornings
hands red, legs cold
slacks and trackies not yet known
spiders' webs along barbed fence
dew-encrusted, shone like diamonds.

On warm mornings we watched for larks
sitting on fence posts.
As we neared they rose in song
spiralling high into the blue
song cascading down.

I have never seen them again
since before I was ten
and still in farmland often pause
scan the fence for tiny birds
listening for their joyful song.

Today, glowing green wheat rolls
sunshine warm as I head north
without thinking I search fences
scan the sky for spiralling larks.

Blue Hills

Serried ranks of rippling ranges
unfold far ahead
at each bend
the hills are just as far away.
Instead of climbing through
the road skirts around…
no definite climb.

I stop on a little rise
far rippling view
framed by bare hills brushed with rust
then far, pale layered blue on blue.

Refreshed, I travel on an hour
and looking back
there are those hills
same serried ranks of blue on blue
rippling, fading
same silhouette that was ahead
now far behind me.
Unknowing, I passed through
those mystical blue mountains.

I wonder
for a while, did I turn blue?

New country

Broken Hill behind me
north from the Barrier Highway
left up the Opal Miner's Way
towards White Cliffs
long dreamed on.

Unknown country
new road for me.

There's something exciting,
magical, mystical
(at least, to me)
setting foot, or wheels
on new country

Not very different to a hundred Ks ago
same flies, wide skies
same crows cawing
but it's new country
so feels different to me
the silence has an unknown quality.

New country enticing me
calling me to come and see.

Leaving Louth

Little river town
pleasant camp by the waterside
under spreading gums.

Friendly country community.
Evening…all gather in the pub
a relaxed family.

I listen to the words flow…
someone sick, needs a hand
a child has a gift for music
needs help to study.
Yes, a family.

Sleep by the river flowing slow
west to the Murray
then the sea.
It has a long, long way to go.

Early morning I'm on the road
heading north-east to the wide outback
one long shadow for every tree
striping the road with gold and black.

Bourke passed by

Bourke eighty miles, the sign said
red dirt road heading north
but that was fifty years ago.

We might never come this way again.
Can't we turn off for just a while
it's not so far
follow that dusty road to Bourke?

No time! No time!
We rolled on east
devouring distances dusty and vast
turn off passed.

Since then I've wondered about Bourke
…the black stump, back of Bourke…
a place of legend and romance
it seemed to me.

And now, at last I've seen Bourke…
nothing mysterious and strange
shops, garages, schools and such
lives lived much as I live mine.

Now, at last
I have been to Bourke.

Shadows across the road

Long drive today…
long dusty run
back to the setting sun
east-north-east along River Road
now coming in to Wanaaring
evening shadows slanting long
end of the day's travelling.

Wherever we go we leave our mark
shadow cast over someone's way.
Perhaps I have made someone sad
something thoughtless I have done…
what shadow did I cast today?

Peace beneath the spreading gums
Paroo River flowing deep.
Near the riverside I camp
and Lord, I pray as I go to sleep
let me leave kind words, a friendly smile
lighten someone's load for a while.

Back on the road with the sun's first ray.

Let me cast a gentle shadow this day
no rubbish to show I came this way.

Another name song

Names of little towns sing to me
calling me to come and see…
Lightning Ridge explored at last
another desire from years long past
then on again to the north-east…
someone in Beenleigh waits for me.

Dirranbandi, Noondoo then Thallon
up to Nindigully on the river Moonie
and another friendly pub community .
Early morning, east for Bungunyah
then Toobeah, Goondiwindi
Bogabilla, Yelarbon
and tidy little Inglewood
coffee and pancakes at Rosie's café
then on to Karera, Warwick way.

Look around town, buy supplies
then head out again north-east
Beaudesert and Boonah next
…been here once, long ago…
then to Beenleigh for a while
and my nephew's friendly smile.

Rain at Cairns, just back from PNG

Last goodbyes over
dear island far behind
now in the past.

Here warm rain
gently caressing
blessing the soil.

Smiling, I remember
warm rain falling there
the children playing

in pools on the grass
dim shadows through
curtains of heavy rain.

Loved memories
of years on Siassi
bless me here
by the Coral Sea
in warm rain falling

Shades of grey

Cairns in the morning…
grey sea
silk rippling
fades into horizon
heaped slate-grey clouds
cumulonimbus
surrounding mountains
grey-misted.
High mackerel sky
shines silver
sleepy sea wrinkles slow.
Salt breeze.

Other skies, far north
look down…
smooth sands of Yaga Bay
sea silk rippling
mountains of New Britain
blue-grey to the east.

Early morning…silken sea
many shades of grey
…so far away.

At Palm Beach

Wind restless,
changeable
blustering
then pleading
dying
then strengthening
lifts my spirit
spiralling, rising
swirling, gusting…
wild wind
salt wind.

On the beachfront
waves crash in
palms thrash
hats fly
souvenir stalls flap
hurriedly vendors pack
tourists head for shelter…

windy day at Palm Beach.

Between again

Last visit to Siassi over
…four weeks submerged
in love and sweet community

singing, laughter and tears
surrounded by lifting seas
sharing memories of years.

Back in Australia, mourning
age and empty coffers
prevent returning.

Between again…torn apart
letting go, changing gears
trying to reclaim my heart.

Verrierdale, green and soft
quiet interlude to unwind
half way home

between wide seas and rolling plains
time to switch my thoughts
back to Australia.

I can do this again
wean my heart away from that loved life
turn back to where God has planted me

…it takes time.

Familiar birdsong

Siassi islands…
manduns' strong sliding call
rising up the valley
screech of klangas.
Kamnese – fish eagles
scream high above.

Birdsong and sound of sea
and I am home
…another home
but no curlews.

Just returned.
Southern Queensland…
feel of home in soft air
intangible sense of place
tethered by birdsong

plovers scrape
racket of parrots, curlew weeping
…more strident, less melodious
than Riverina curlews
but still curlews
essence of my childhood.

I'm ready now to head for home
Bound for South Australia.

Soft country

I'll store these…
miles of glowing green
stretched rolling to the sea
country roads ribboning
towns half glimpsed
where I have never been
hidden in hills
embraced by dusty scrub
and groves of pine

I'll store these…
humming living silences
green singing wheat
wayside swaying grasses
graceful white oats
caw of crows
distant hum of traffic…
I will store them in my heart.

West into the interior now…
a different beauty.

Divided Loyalty

Hot eucalypt hush
crows' cries, blowflies
and deep inland silence
grasp my heart.
but also ordered aisles of pines,
meadows manicured and lush.

Bare brown inland
ochre rocks, red dust
and stony plains I love
also green rounded hills
old, gnarled orchards
and wide wheat fields
skies arched high above
and this…wide skies, eagle soaring
fierce mountain wind reaching forever
tumbled farmhouse, solitary pepper tree
…and this
wide brown landscape
low hills, stretching far…caw of crow
plaintive curlew's wail under evening star
…and these leafy suburban streets
redolent of gracious living
trees overarching
this too.
My heart has space.

Nindigully on the Moonie River

Sun sets in a glory of red and gold
heaped clouds lined with flame and rust
as I head up the darkening road
to Nindigully.

It was my plan to be driving south
but no way through on these backtracks
so a detour north to find a camp
at Nindigully.

Sun sinks slow and the world is black
ghost kangaroos drift across the track
as I bore on towards my rest
at Nindigully.

Friendly people, local blokes
country music, laughter, jokes
it's good to be with country folks
at Nindigully.

Returning campers exchanging tips
sharing the high points of their trips.
I hope to come back some day
to friendly Nindigully.

Roadkill

I'm not about to get poetic about well-dead bodies
swollen, stinking, assaulting all senses
or long gone, bits of bone, ribcage open to the sky
no, they don't inspire me
or emus…aristocratic, skirts flouncing delicately
but nothing elegant about a well-dead emu
brindled feather scattered haphazardly
dark flesh, dark blood…it's a mess
or pigs, legs pointing to the sky…they don't inspire me.

This is about kangaroos, symbol of Australia
bounding gracefully through the outback
dozing under shady tree beside the track
dim mob floating over darkening road
or standing poised, watching me pass
ears twitching, nose sniffing…fastidious.

By the road next morning many lie
little hands raised beseeching to the sky,
Why did this happen to me?
How will my little one live without me?
…so many 'roos dead by the road
raptors must eat but can't keep up…
many orphan joeys who will not survive
so be careful when you drive…especially at night.

Keep safe. Don't speed. Rest. Survive.
and keep your eyes scanning side to side.

Let's aim for less roadkill.

Dareel to Dingadee

1846 to 1958 the sign says
here was a tiny town
not far from Mungindi
on the River Moonie.
This little village, home to families
a wide world to children
wonder in every bend and tree.

The coach came through
with bugle and flourish
bustle and flurry
life blood of the town.
Now. quiet, dry
houses gone
a few rusted tools
broken stone walls falling down.
I took a rusted link of chain
in memory of you, Dareel.

Now on to Dingadee
wheat short, hardly any stalk
merciless sky
black soil cracked and dry
drunken fence fragments lie
wire rusted and slack
land flat, so flat
gates leaning awry.

No skylarks here…
on to South Australia.

On the road again

Early morning on the road
Adelaide hills behind me
out into the flat country

orange sun low through the trees
fingers paddocks
caresses close-cropped wheat
everything golden
warm and welcoming
sharp stubble softened to velvet

mellow morning sunlight
slanting soft, cool yellow
across the fields.

An hour's driving
now sun is up, light strong
still the shadows are long
sunlight striped gold
on fields green and glowing.

Magical red gold sunrise past
day begins.

Near Karoonda

Tall pink grass swaying
tender as young mushrooms gills
or a pale, pale salmon rose
the bottom of a baby's feet…
gentle blend of all of those.

Pink? I must find another word…
fading evening sunset cloud
galahs' feathers in the breeze…
there must be a word more true
to this gentle yet vibrant hue than pink.

Greens…olive greens, shadow greens
the fresh, bright green of spring
clean green of rain-washed mallee leaves
their tips that same tender pink!

Creams…ripe oats' heads, soft white lace
delicate as a wedding dress
filigree edging the road
pale against the swaying fields
weaving dreams against the greens.

There have been plentiful rains.
In summer, dry and dusty plains
now verdant with glowing tender greens
and vernal seed heads swaying

Cinnamon-pink tenderness…
yes, that's it! The colour is the same
as new, pink tips on cinnamon trees.
Even that does not sound quite right.
I'll have to try again.

Passed by

I passed by you in the night
it was late
didn't stop
rolled on along the road.

Perhaps I was wrong
perhaps I was right.
I had come a long way
had a long way still to go.

You would have pressed me to stay
and so lose another day.
I felt tendrils reaching for me
felt your presence not far away.

I would have loved to see your face
to sit and chat with you a space
but it was late
you were asleep
and I had promises to keep
and a long way yet to go
and so…

I passed by you in the night
and you didn't know.

Little Desert

River red gums
solid, timeless
leaves shining
shimmering
turning
in morning sunlight.

Breeze cool
peaceful pool…
horizontal ripples
reeds perpendicular
lush, plush
rise from still water.

Reeds rustle
distant bird song
hawk soars…

gentle morning
at Little Desert.

For a stranger met in Dimboola

Your father, recently left this world
…known face, long loved
but behind the face
so much unseen, unsuspected.

My father, known and loved
but at his funeral surprises unveiled.

You regret you never knew
your father's love of jazz…at his funeral
a friend played in memory
of jazz session after meetings.
You grieve that you didn't know
this facet of his character.

Funerals…mourning and discovery
unsuspected threads
surprising pages rise from tears.

Familiar country town often passed…
behind the shops and houses
an unknown world.
Winding paths among river gums
ancient homesteads
fascinating debris of lives
piles of rusty, broken machinery…
treasure trove hidden behind the known.

Between Minyip and St Arnaud

As I pass
spirit fingers reach out from deserted homes
across dusty fields quiet voices call to me…
My life has been full of wonder
I wouldn't change with anyone
but as I pass through this dusty land
I feel a loss…here was a community
a life never known to me.
As I pass, their spirits call.

And did those children who call to me
who lived long ago in this dry, wide land
live lives of delight and discovery
in this wonderful world of theirs
little corners, treasures and mysteries?
Did they, as I, search for shining beetles
build caves and castles and Indian forts
dreaming, building memories
while their parents faced defeat?

I pass through the dusty land and wonder
where did those children go…
to the cities…or to the cemetery
to positions of importance or to obscurity…
happy, fulfilled lives…who knows?

Their spirits whisper to me
of a child's full life lived here.

I whisper back to them,
I was a child. Still am. I understand.

Homesteads

North of Bendigo, homesteads nestle
embedded in sheds and embracing trees.

I envy them, as I pass
their settled life with family
place in this community
ties that will last
and perhaps they look at me
as I drive by
with resentment or jealousy
wishing they could be
travelling free.

We each are tied in some ways
husband, children, work
perhaps enjoy life's hectic race
but still
sometimes dream of being free
of things we'd like to do
envying other's lives
imagined through our own world view

probably inaccurate
because you are not me
and I am not you.

Lonely Road

Only me on the road today
mallee whips by, clouds whip by
birds soar high in windy sky
the road is mine alone
rolling on enticingly.

Grey day on the road today
clouds pressing down
rain rattling down
loose gravel blasts
batters undercarriage.
car vibrates all day
water on window whirling
low land dim and grey.

A brisk day on the road today.
We squeeze between land and sky
thrusting through showers and mist
while paddocks half seen roll by
windscreen blurred and muddy.

No hope of larks today.

Tooleybuc

I crossed the river at Tooleybuc
sweet little river town
rattled over the wooden bridge
found a corner to settle down.

I slept high on the bank
above the stream
watching the river flow
the dark water's gleam
silently sliding, slipping
quiet gurgle and plop
slow flow glinting, shining
smooth as silk on top
but subtle pleating
betraying secrets below

current under the surface
boiling, roiling
caressing something
deep beneath
as the deceitful surface
murmurs quietly

relentless onward flow
implacable.

What is hidden below?

Discovering Barham

Fire siren at 5.30, so up and off
eat my last apple as I cross the bridge
changing song over centre section
gateway for river boats long ago.

Through the streets to sense the town
then right to follow Lake Boga sign
which I'm sure will link to Deniliquin road
through stately Barham forest
…been this way many years ago.

Winding road, lush river flats
fattening cattle and orange groves
a paddock full of Berkshire pigs
running to meet me, hoping for food
hundreds of black pigs line the fence
pleading with me as I drive by.

Barham Forest road is closed
so back along the winding track
knowing this corner a little better
envying the lives lived there
a foolish habit I have…
back past the cows and excited pigs
caravan park and green, green fields
and right for Deniliquin.

Another corner explored
and stored.

Deniliquin on the Edward River

Solid
prosperous
familiar red-brick banks and offices.
I found a friendly restaurant
…slow hot coffee ..

Noted
as the birthplace
the home of Malcolm Fraser
and many years before he lived
the Berapa Beraba.

Handsome
proud patriarchs
hotels watch over all
as in other Riverina towns
of memory

I desire
to spend time here
sadly must pass quickly through
leaving Deniliquin behind
still much unknown.

On to Henty.

Wet day on Hay Plains

Humming drumming
engine thrumming
whirlpools on wind screen
dark paddocks dimly seen
Henty, I am coming.

Road leads on, on
to the dim horizon.
Follow, follow the white line
through stormy, writhing dark…
tunnelling between mallee and pine.

Evening descending
closes in, darkening
unrolling road misting, vanishing
rare, lonely homesteads glow
folded into hollows.

At last horizon lightens
out into feeble sun
clouds gone
storm done.

I stop a few times to sit and listen
search the sky
but it's not weather for birds.
No larks sing
no larks fly.

Tracking myself on the map

East from Adelaide
over the South Australia border
into Victoria for a while.

Murrayville, Banka, Underbool, Walpeup
Ouyen, Manangatang, Piangil
and how could I miss Tooleybuc?
Nyah, Swan Hill, Kerang, Koondrook
then across the Murray at Barham bridge
exploring river towns unknown to me
along the waterfront, majestic trees
and the river flowing relentlessly.

Deniliquin, Blighty, Finley, Berrigen
Oakdale…trees shift shape…more familiar
Urana now not far away.
Eastwards, on towards my birth town
Bidgeemia, Urangeline, Pleasant Hills
not one lark heard today.

Now trees change to box and native pine
a different quality of air and light
loose screws, puzzle pieces
click in to their places…
almost my home country.

An intriguing little lane

Dusty lane beckons under arching gums
winds out of sight

galahs squabble above, parrots whistle
pigeons take flight

dry grasses dance in gentle inland breeze
skirts lacy white…

lane twists and turns, disappears round the bend
beckoning me.

those straight laneways of the unchanging plains
ordinary…

this small winding track near Urangeline
has mystery.

twisting on between native pines, calling
Come, follow me.

Heading for Henty

Nearing Oakdale, country changes
still flat, but different trees
not my heart's country as yet…
suggestion of foothills to the east.

Past Yerong Creek
all seems right
something inside clicks into place
sights and smells fit a waiting space…
deep inside my being
something settles and sighs.

Nearer…familiar encircling hills
groves of wattles and sturdy box
sprinkle of native pines
avenues of sugar gums

Munyabla siding
and there…
Waldeck home gates welcoming me
far Rock silhouetted bold
matching the imprint on my mind.

This land my father loved, and wrestled
forced by inexorable events to leave
has a rightness in my eyes above all other
…those dear places where I have lived.

Little town

Little town
drowsing in morning sun
cat basking on the path
yellow leaves
rich autumn air.

We left…
and lost so much.

Where we went
was meant to be
but if we'd stayed
how different
life could have been

We lost continuity
so I'm a visitor
in my home town
welcomed, embraced
by wide morning streets.

If we'd stayed…
but we took a different road
so
Hello there, little town
familiar and strange
air alive with could-have-beens
and, too soon, goodbye again.

Old Woodlorne Homestead

I picked a rose for Auntie Gertie
and some evening primrose plants
from the derelict garden where she reigned
to plant in mine, in her memory.
Her impeccable house, empty for years
a sad shell…
I explored the dusty farmyard
long grasses and crowding thistles
searching for souvenirs
a few links of old chain
a piece of harness?
But all was bare.
No souvenirs there.

Breeze sad through the pepper trees
emptiness where there was busy life
chooks, turkeys and kangaroo dogs
busy pig yards and sheep pens
and our favourite uncle, chuckling.

Gone, familiar voices
fascinating jumble of machinery.
Pathway from Woodlorne to Waldeck
our old home
fenced off, overgrown
unrecognisable.

Retracing childhood pathways
impossible.

Listening near Munyabla

So still by the old church site.
Inland wind remains the same
speaking gently in the trees
roadside oats still whispering
echoes of congregation singing
cicadas buzz.
Far south the familiar sentinel Rock
against pale skies.

Thank you, Lord, for this place
our time in this sacred space…
red-brick church long gone
Your word lives on.

I listen, searching fence posts.
Where are the larks?

Avenues of box, wattles and pine…
what has this road seen?
I drive slowly where we rode our bikes
in memory of singing larks
childhood wonder and exploration…
paused by Lieschkes to listen again
and at sad empty site of Edgehill school
a wheat field now where lined trees say
here was once a school
where now childhood spirits play.

Not even one lark heard, but soon
warmth and tears and laughter
in my hometown.

A Macreadie

Macreadie!
Macreadie!
I've met a Macreadie!
Someone who knew
the western borders of my childhood
territory forboding, enticing.

Those dark pines, brooding, mysterious
out of bounds over Macreadie's fence
lured us far over the stubble to trespass.
Exotic pine needle carpet and buried bones!
Dark and sinister…imagined groans!

The Macreadies saw it from the other side.
We never met…hid, fearing discovery

probably this delicious mystery
was all in our minds
Mother's instructions to stay close to home
blown out of proportion
grown into this fantasy.

Now, at last, over sixty years later
I have met a Macreadie…
a momentous day for me.

Ah, Josephine

Josephine
we will sleep beside the river
listening to the speaking trees.

Ah, Josephine
you are all I hoped for
practical, not pretty
not low to the road
high enough for country tracks
and OK in the city.

Josephine
just the right size for me
room to sleep and room to carry
all I need to camp and travel
to fossick, noodle and explore.

Only a machine, it's true
but we have travelled far together
slept beside many streams.

We suit each other, Josephine.

In search of a stony stream

Brown dams and creeks were all we knew
and seldom ventured somewhere new.
Waldeck was our world.

Our one family holiday
we camped at Bright
clear fresh water flowing
coloured stones glowing
scent of pines, a different light.
We slept on bracken fern
in the back of our truck
fragrant nights
days dreamed past building dams
redirecting streams.

Back home we went to brown water
stagnant, slow-flowing.

Later we lived by the Onkaparinga
clear, fresh water over stones
curving round boulders…living
stones rich and glowing
water sculpted, moulded.

A deep love grew in me
for clear, running water
always yearning to return
to clean streams
with wet stones glowing.

Somewhere north of Beechworth

Northwards, northwards…
it seems forever
twisted maze of tracks behind.
Wrong turn somewhere…a mistake?
Perhaps, but heady wine
to be alone in new country
the tangled scrub, my car and me
the sun my only sign.

North, forever north…
will I eventually be found
long expired from misadventure…
can't you see the bold headline?
No, I have water still, aplenty
food and fuel and all I need
and this my dream, to venture far
delicious mix…excitement and fear.
Will I find my way out?

Northwards, it seems forever…
this is Old Coach Road, I think
new road conquered, so never mind
ahead, I know, two highways link.
Beechworth now far behind
I surrender to the rocky track.

No going back.

Corryong

I slept high on Corryong lookout
rising from the plains
air cool and pleasant as I hoped
days here dry, sultry, hot

Morning fresh and cool
Murray River spread below
sun rising over the mountains
far slice of hopeful pink and blue
under dark sky
higher clouds limned with gold
lower fading, fading
into ominous grey…
probably a rainy day.

I will watch sunrise in this new place
then go down to the town below
find a hot drink
record my thoughts and think
where next…
and what this journey is teaching me.

Here was a church

Crowded gums mark old boundaries
broken bricks scattered
a few decrepit graves…
a hallowed patch of ground
where once a church flourished
people gathered each Sunday
from farms around

…and nearby another site
marked by angular pines
bending together to whisper
their lost history…
perhaps a school?
I hear children's voices.
Inland wind bends the dry grass
as pale pageants pass.

Gnarled and twisted trees
huddle to gossip
and mourn days gone.

Over the Divide

The reed-tufted meadows I've longed to see
marshy streams, twisted snow gums
where we sang Settler's songs
and 'Bound for South Australia'
on our wandering way home from PNG
almost fifty years ago.

Snowy scheme descendants
enrich this mountainous area
the high Kiandra plains, Adaminaby
where wild horses roamed free
immortalised in settlers' songs
fixed firmly in my memory…

Will I ever again visit that country
those wild, high plains east of the divide
…deep grass waving, golden paddocks
strewn with ice-moulded boulders
heavy menacing clouds overhead
dark against sunlit land.

…through Cabramatta, years ago
the highest school in Australia
then over the divide
wind down the other side
heading for Tumbarumba
then back to Henty.

In search of Gold

Reedy creek, Beechworth…dry as a bone
dust and gravel and stone
I meant to scoop gravel beneath the falls
but only stagnant, dirty pools
with leeches…repulsive…so it's clear
I couldn't seek my fortune there.

I had searched on Google, found a spot.
near Tumbarumba's western slopes
Sapphires, rubies, garnets, gold
that is the story Google told.

I studied the map, sought those streams
four times, five times followed a track
and each time it was the same
blackberries, impenetrable,
soon turned me back.
To access the stream…impossible…
so no paddling, no rubies, garnets, gold.

Nothing so delicious as blackberries
in pies or jam, of course with cream
but these vines rampage unchecked
natural beauties overrun…
no streamlets singing in the sun
nowhere to pan for gold.

Home…mind full of Alpine scenes
hills and rivers and laughing streams
to satisfy my inner eyes
fuel future dreams and verse and sighs
but no gemstones or gold for me…
foiled by leeches and blackberries.

Near Tumbarumba

Menacing dark cloud
waiting, waiting…
I rise up the hill
spider crouching
grotesque, glaring
stalking me
crawling closer, closer.

Under I go.
Spider's fangs
dissolve in rain.
wipers frantic
visibility low
I inch along
rain shouting, roaring
maelstrom surrounding
car secure and warm.
Josephine and I
insulated
encapsulated
safe under the storm

…then out the other side.
Frowning dark the cloud crawls on
seeking new victims to prey upon
still swollen with a load
for unwary travellers…
leaving Josephine shining clean
on the sunny, steaming road.

Henty again

Small town flows past
wanderers and overtakers
clumps gather, chatter
call across the wide street
Most don't know me
…perhaps remember my family.

It's so familiar to be here.
We meet, share news and memories
but there's a chasm between
their lives and mine…
I went away.

Close country families
in each other's daly history
shared years, trials and victories
are outside my reality.

Although I wouldn't change my life
still I feel a loss.

At Nag Nag Wah campsite

Camping at Nag Nag by the creek
deep in trees at Buffalo's feet
water shining, rippling, singing
chuckling over stones and logs.
I feast on fried potatoes and crays
and a mug of Zweck's Tokay
sit on the bank in the evening sun
stream's murmur mesmerising me
unknowing, carefree
beginning its journey to the sea.

The end of another travelling day
rich with trees and sky and stream
a pancake lunch with berries and cream
now I sit by the laughing water and dream
as I sip sweet, rich Tokay
and Lord I pray
for all those in detention, in cages and prisons
of laws or sickness or sorrow or fear
that they could one day be blessed like me
with time to know a flowing stream
to cleanse their souls and carry their dreams.

Crossroads

Bandiana, Leneva, Staghorn Flat
Wooragee
Baarmutha, Murmangee
Beechworth, Myrtleford, Eurobin
Porepunkah and Bright.
Mountain air misty blue and clean
grass grows long and lush and green
comfortable homesteads nest
among tangled orchards and sheds
but I must turn west.

That road goes on to Germantown
Harrietville, Hotham, then south
or perhaps I could cross over
to the Kiewa River Valley…
Mt Beauty, Bogong then Falls Creek
Dinner Plains, Anglers Rest
explore the Omeo road…
all in dreams as yet
…strange names calling me.

I turn from dreams and wind to the west.
Dadongadale, Cheshunt, Whitfield, Myrrhee
rejoin the highway at Benalla.
Goodbye for now to the high country
…so many places still to see
to feel the touch of each one's soul.

Treasures mount up but never fill
my heart.
I'm hungry still.

Mountain Song

I have felt the mountain's breath
the mountain's tears
the mountain's song is in my ears
wind, bird cries and rushing streams
and now it seems
I must return to the flat and wide
and home calls as I westward ride
heart full of mountain dreams.

This flat land has beauty too
features more subtle, browner hue
and if I lived in that mountainous place
I might long to return to this flat, brown land
far views, distant horizons, space
perhaps…
but now
my heart resounds with a different song…
how could I stay from the mountains so long?

Soon I will turn back to to the highlands again
to refresh my spirit
inspire my pen.

Reflections

At Lameroo, almost home
another road trip almost done
I pause back in the flat country
for a peaceful day with family.

A quiet house, a moody breeze
wide windows, swaying trees
I hear the birds, and see them pass
hear the wind caress the grass
tall pines moving gracefully.
I have ears to hear, and eyes to see…
my Lord, you are so good to me.

As the road unrolls, the miles slide by
under the wide Australian sky
I follow my dreams to places new
always more to see and do…
health and wealth and I am free.
My Lord, you are so good to me.

Blackbirds stealing mulberries
sweet silence and slow-moving trees
heart to feel and mind to roam
as long as this earth is my home.

You have blessed me generously.
My Lord, you are so good to me.

The magic of maps

I gaze on a map and questions rise
places untouched draw my eyes
a name springs out, magnifies, glows
in my mind a fantasy grows
who lives there, what rivers rise
are there skylarks in those skies?

Place names are only words
but reading them my heart is stirred
to know that place, its history
to store in my memory.

Maps call…places I have known
convey love and memories
those still unvisited, unknown
are intriguing mysteries.

Names engraved on my heart
places where I have lived
each one an integral part
of my identity…

Fascinating to me
the life inside a map.

www.ingramcontent.com/pod-product-compliance
Lightning Source LLC
Chambersburg PA
CBHW062139100526
44589CB00014B/1626